To

Adèle.

Lot's of love from Mum.

I will love you until
The sea's run dry
and time stands still

ANCHOR BOOKS

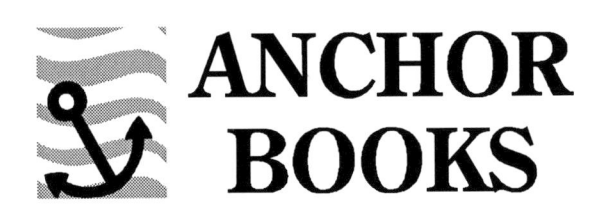

IT'S FUNNY WHEN...

Edited by

Heather Killingray

First published in Great Britain in 2002 by
ANCHOR BOOKS
Remus House,
Coltsfoot Drive,
Peterborough, PE2 9JX
Telephone (01733) 898102

All Rights Reserved

Copyright Contributors 2002

HB ISBN 1 84418 062 X
SB ISBN 1 84418 063 8

*F*OREWORD

Anchor Books is a small press, established in 1992, with the aim of promoting readable poetry to as wide an audience as possible.

We hope to establish an outlet for writers of poetry who may have struggled to see their work in print.

The poems presented here have been selected from many entries, and as always editing proved to be a difficult task.

I trust this selection will delight and please the authors and all those who enjoy reading poetry.

Heather Killingray
Editor

CONTENTS

Lady Of Leisure	Deborah Jane Mailer	1
Lament For A Laptop	Richard Young	2
Grin And Declare It!	Dennis Overton	3
Anyone For Tennis?	Margaret East	6
Untitled	Linda Doel	7
The Inquisitive Male!	Brian Akers	8
Holiday Preparations	Val Hessey	9
The Best Medicine	Jane Milthorp	10
The Lion's Dinner	Anne Elibol	11
Untitled	Jason Wilde	12
Limerick	Michael Fenton	13
Millicent Mann	David Isaac	14
The Fly	Sonia Riggs	15
The Little Things That Add Up In Life	Albert Russo	16
Comedy And God	Kenneth Mood	18
The Luncheon Club	Keith Allison	19
Comparing Notes	Ruth Cargill	20
Do You Know Your Angels?	Milan Trubarac	21
My Mammy	Janet Petchey	22
Butterfly	Keith B Osborne	23
The Long Night	G M Baker	24
Pigs With A Taste Of Gallic	Celia G Thomas	25
Whimsically Weird	George S Johnstone	26
Sorry I Didn't Mean To - It Was An Accident	Louise King	27
Untitled	Brenda Hill	28
The School Run	Sharron Rushton	29
My Holiday In Spain	Ennis	30
Lost And Found	Laura Harris	31
Aye Aye Captain	Ronald D Lush	32
Kids	Ruth Chignell-Stapleton	33
Teenage Boys	Julie Livett	34
Food	Paul Duddles	36
Last Will And Testament	Muriel Reed	37
Helianthus Annuus	Betty Nevell	38

Vacation	Milly Hatcher	39
Humour	G Nicklin	40
I Bought A Book	Patricia Mullins	41
Principal Fear	Nigel Stanley	42
The Doctor's Surgery	Pearl Stebbings	43
Wish You Were Here	Norma Rudge	44
Ode To Naomi	Becky Garrett	45
Supergirl's Cat	Peter Coulter	46
Friday Night	John Foster	47
Briny Whiting	Philip Beverley	48
Untitled	Marjorie Grant	49
One Monday Morning	Maureen Ayling	50
If Pigs Could Fly	Barry Clist	52
A Musical Mystery	Roger Williams	53
Meniere's Disease	V M McKinley	54
Three's A Crowd	Dorothy Elthorne-Jones	55
Not Too Sure	Fred Norgrove	56
About Me	Pleione Tooley	58
The Prince And The Corgi	Kathy Rawstron	59
Boys Will Be Boys	Joan Hammond	60
Diddle, Diddle, Dumpling	E M Higgins	61
Greens	G F Watts	62
Easy Does It	E A Evans	63
Night-Time Ramblings	Alister H Thompson	64
Nanny And Hazel	Adam Teeling	65
The Outsize Family	John Townend	66
Age	Gaynor Florence Perry	67
The Eco Warrior	Linda A Knight	68
The Tax Man	Daniel Jack	69
Bray	Alan Seaward	70
The Truce	Hilda Ellis	71
Those Austrian Blinds	Carol Ann Darling	72
The Carer	Betty Smyth	73
Daddy's Train Set	Joyce Walker	74
Where Are The Roses?	Kathleen M Hatton	75
A Good Catch	Stan Gilbert	76
Monsterman	Louise Lee	77
My Knight	Hazel Mills	78

The Wedding	Elizabeth Hiddleston	79
My Dilemma	Ivy Stewart	80
Hill Walking On Mars	Alice Rawlinson	81
Tickled Pink	S Glover	82
Making The Bed	Joanna Pickett	83
Lippy Limerick	Joanne Wilcock	84
Pigs Might Fly	Ruth Morris	85
On First Looking Into People's Humour	D M Anderson	86
Limerick	Barrie Williams	87
Laughing Leslie	Christine Hardemon	88
Husband's New Shorts	Pamela Carder	89
Cassius Clay	E Gosney	90
The Jumble Sale	S A Baker	91
My Friend Gillian	May Ward	92
The Razzle Dazzler	L Nokes	93
Humour	Mary Chadwick	94
Wally Wimpole	John Wayre	95
The Black Cat	Marie Barker	96
In The Supermarket	Michael Rowson	97
Bank Holiday	Doris Lilian Critchley	98
God's Special Days	Colin Allsop	99
Summer Fate	Vann Scytere	100
Sparks	Grant Sulkin	101
The Shoe Shop Girl	Marian Voice Gifford	102
It Was A Funny Thing	Phil Aylward	103
There And Back	Camillia Zedan	104
The Best Medicine	Jo Taylor	105
Get Together If You Can	Joyce Atkinson	106
High Function	Terence Leslie	107
The Avocado	Katherine Parker	108
Oh! Innocence	Jim Pritchard	109
A Light Shower	Margaret Carter	110
Johnny Bull	Jane Margaret Isaac	111
Elderberry Wine	Olive M Poole	112
Jenny Hen	Marion Skelton	113
Yorkshire Pudding	Evelyn Balmain	114

LADY OF LEISURE

I'm a lady of leisure now,
Or so my husband says.
When he runs off to work at dawn,
I get to stay in bed.
He doesn't think about the kids,
That fall out of bed at eight.
He doesn't worry about the rush
To stop them being late.
At ten when he goes on his break,
I'm usually making beds.
At twelve when someone serves him lunch,
I'm polishing stair heads.
At one o'clock I wash the clothes,
At two I walk the dog.
At three I walk to get the kids
In rain, hail, sleet and fog.
At four I hoover - once again,
At five I make the dinner.
At six I run the children's bath
And throw clothes in the spinner.
When people ask me what I do,
Inside I smile with pleasure,
For the only reply that I can give
Is, I'm a lady of leisure.

Deborah Jane Mailer

LAMENT FOR A LAPTOP

I used to have a laptop
To help me in my work:
I didn't have to pay for it;
It was a business perk.

I swallowed all the sales spiel
And the media hype about
Increasing productivity
And giving business 'clout.'

I read up on the literature
And had many sleepless nights
Trying to get my head round
'Megahertz' and 'gigabytes.'

I tried to type up my reports,
And spell-checked what I'd say,
But the darned thing was American
And spelled everything *its* way.

Then I tried to use a spreadsheet
To work out my accounts,
But I must have got a formula wrong
Cos I got some strange amounts.

I thought I'd do a slide show
That would move on at a click:
It should have, but it didn't
And that really made me sick!

I logged on to our network
But found it had been hacked:
Still, at least there's justice;
The IT manager's been sacked.

So, (you're probably there before me,
For you've followed this no doubt)
I opened up *my* windows
And I threw the blighter out!

Richard Young

GRIN AND DECLARE IT!

In order to outline, clarify and confirm the content of a
                                        widespread rumour,
The next budget will include a revenue imposed on humour.
Our policy is simple, all conversation and social topics
                                        aimed to lift the blues
Are subject to a well constructed, regulated, scale of dues.
Any display of inspired, ingenious wit, amiable banter
                                        or jovial repartee
Will qualify for payment of the appropriate, approved and
                                        appointed fee.
New legislation relating to the charge on merriment and light-
                                        hearted jest
Is linked to government bonds in which the morose and
                                        miserable can invest.
Photographs portraying happy, joyful gatherings and endearing smiles,
For collection purposes, are to be compiled on the
                                  'Ministry of Misery' files.
(The majority of people identified are most likely classified as
                                        tax exiles.)
At election time, financial gain derived from this new levy on laughs
Will be clearly recorded and displayed on 'Money Milked
                                        From Mirth' graphs.
We feel Parliament can rejoice at this fresh source of very
                                        welcome income,
To quote a colloquial saying, input for the coffers classed
                                        as 'Fair Dinkum.'
To enforce these rules, comic interaction noted by
                                        strategically placed detectors
Will be transmitted to surly inspectors, installed prominently
                                        e sectors.
Prime Ministers and official nominees are fully exempt,
                                        ort a beaming grin,
An advertisement for dental care, privileged position, and
                                        ity to spin.

A gesture of goodwill, made to anyone who thinks this an
                                             on humour
Constitutes a pint of bitter, bunch of sour grapes, and an
                                             ripe satsuma.
Higher rate payers who, after much effort, cannot restrain
                                             from jocular vein
Are granted a concession allowing a fortnight of fun-filled
                                             frolic in Spain.
If you find these proposals an intrusion or further increase in
                                             political bloomers
Criticism must not be interpreted in terms equivalent to 'verbal
                                             Montezuma's'
Laughter, the best medicine; oh please, what a joke, come off it,
Do you realise pharmaceutical companies would accumulate
                                             far less profit?
If any reader considers our intention amusing, after this
                                             statement perusing,
Save some coin, do not smirk, such sentiment instantly rescind.
Specify your facial gesture was merely a consequence of
                                             unsuppressible wind!

Dennis Overton

ANYONE FOR TENNIS?

Anyone for tennis?
It's such a lovely day.
Anyone for tennis?
Who would like to play?

My racquet's newly strung,
My shorts are very short,
My partner's looking handsome,
New balls are on the court.

And now we start,
I serve a double fault,
Then I serve another.
My partner looks distraught.

We play for half an hour,
Losing every game.
I look towards my partner,
He doesn't look the same.

For now he's very angry,
He kicks away the ball.
Now he's really steaming,
His racquet hits the wall.

I try to make excuses
About playing in my heyday,
He looks at me aghast.
Oh damn it! Anyone for croquet?

Margaret East

UNTITLED

There was a young man from France
Who stuffed socks down the front of his pants
The reason for this
To enlarge his bits
And excite the ladies of dance.

Linda Doel

THE INQUISITIVE MALE!

This man climbed up a tree by rope
To look at the landscape through a telescope,
And when up the tree he cried, 'I can see!'
'See what?' called his wife from below.
His life of 60 years did bestow,
She said, 'You're far too old to be climbing trees!
Besides, there's a nest full of bees!'
'What?' he said, with alarm,
'Ouch! One just stung my right arm.'
'All right,' his wife said,
'You've got one left,'
And as he began to descend,
The branch with the rope on began to bend!
And the bees started swarming around.
'Let go of the rope,' his wife shouted,
And he fell 20 feet to the ground.
He lay there in a human heap,
His wife dialled 999,
The ambulance was there in three minutes flat,
They said, 'Sorry, we ran over your cat.'
They took him away.
She said, 'It's time for bed.
What an interesting day!'

Brian Akers

HOLIDAY PREPARATIONS

The fridge has been emptied, the floors have been cleaned.
The hustle and bustle, you've never dreamed.
The windows are shining clear and bright
The doors have been locked, security's tight.

We've cancelled the milk and the papers too.
There's always something more to do.
We've checked the tickets again and again
I know the currency is not the same.

The taxi is waiting, we turn off the lights
I think we're ready to take our flight.
Our holiday's starting, excitement is mounting
There's too much luggage, well we're not counting.

We take our seats, the plane is full
It won't take long - it's not long haul.
While we're there, there is so much to do
Swimming and walking and dancing too.

When the holiday is over, money spent
Knowing we shall have to pay the rent,
We'll do it again, as we've always done
Just for two glorious weeks in the hot, hot sun.

Val Hessey

THE BEST MEDICINE

Minnie and Jimmy
Were two of a kind,
Small, with a large behind.

Jane Milthorp

THE LION'S DINNER

John entered the cage
He stood brave and bold
But what was to happen
Could not be foretold.

At the crack of his whip
The lions assembled
Upon their high stools
Grand kings they resembled.

At first things went well
The lions obeyed
But unknown to John
The leader had strayed.

John's biggest mistake
Was in turning his back
Not watching the leader
In charge of the pack.

The lion, it didn't hesitate
So before John could turn
It was a minute too late
The lion had him pinned to the floor
Then at John's head, he began to gnaw.

Women, they screamed
Children, they cried
To see the remains that lay inside
The lion mistook John for some beef
So all that remained
Were John's false teeth!

Anne Elibol

UNTITLED

One day at the fair a young hobo named Mo
Strolled too near the stage and hit his toe
Oh no! He tripped into the act but
Somersaulted over onto his back.
Ho ho! People laughed and clapped,
They thought Mo was part of the show.

Jason Wilde

LIMERICK

There was a young man from Hong Kong
whose ambition was to strike a big gong
he never forgave the Brits
for so easily calling it quits
now he's famous for playing Mah-jong in a thong.

Michael Fenton

MILLICENT MANN

Millicent Mann owned a vending machine
Which would sell anything the colour of green
Bottles all hanging, ten in a row
Sniffles and snot from up someone's nose
A one-eyed monster called jealousy
The after effect of sickness at sea
Grass, hedgerows, lettuce and parrots
Did I mention in the sea-sick
There were, of course, carrots
A vending machine owned by Millicent Mann
Uprooted, migrated, re-housed in Greenland.

David Isaac

THE FLY

Whilst wandering through the park,
A fly pitched on my nose,
'Hello,' I said through two boss eyes,
'And how does your life go?'

Sonia Riggs

THE LITTLE THINGS THAT ADD UP IN LIFE

At our first appointment I came a little early
I remember the afternoon being a little too hot
and I felt a little depressed
the moment we met I sensed she'd expected someone a little younger
she'd found me a little too lonely and
believed I needed a little extra personal care
and before I could say 'zoooo' we'd moved into a little apartment

in the beginning we both earned very little money
doing odd jobs and little nothings
but little did we worry in those days
where small was still beautiful
and littler even better
then she grew a little tired of me
and we got into each other's way
a little more every passing day
she said I'd become a little too lazy
so she yelled at me like crazy
and began to think very little of me
in the meantime, we'd managed to produce a child
at birth he was so little I was scared to hold him
that's when she claimed I knew little or nothing about life
and that if I hadn't been the baby's father
she would not need me around
adding after each row: 'for the little that you do for us!'

How about now, you will ask, well things have changed a little
she puts the music a little too loud
wears her rouge a little too red
walks a little too fast
pouts a little too often
she's a little overweight
watches TV a little too late
sleeps a little too long

and still finds the time to fight
she buys little food that I like
so that when I go to bed I always feel a little hungry
she dons blouses a little too tight
and that makes me a little jealous
especially when she talks to that little twerp of a mailman
now that the kid walks, our place is a little too small
but she acts as though I were little more than a ghost.

See what happens when you realise things a little too late!

Albert Russo

COMEDY AND GOD

Des O'Connor and Ken Dodd
Make me laugh out loud.
Over the years they have
Cheered me up when I have
Been down in the mud.
It's true, laughter
Is the best medicine.

So, come everybody,
Smile for family and friends.
There you see, your eyes
Are full of love and joy.
Pray for me now
And I'll pray for Anchor Books
Staff and writers.

Kenneth Mood

THE LUNCHEON CLUB

It's here, it's here, the luncheon club is here!
We've waited many a fretful week
Just to hear our Tina speak these words -
The luncheon club is here!

They carry a varied menu,
There's something for every taste,
For cannibals there's the pigmies,
And for pigmies there's the waste!

We started off with crusty bread
All nicely edged with green,
But Eileen said, 'Not to worry,
It's been rubbed with a kidney bean'

We saved a little of our crust for eating with our soup,
A lentil broth that made you heave
Until you could yourself relieve,
But it stops you getting croup!

Dessert was nice, they said plum duff
That's what they told us all,
They'd garnished it with plaster
From off the kitchen wall!

The tea and coffee were superb,
Recognised straight away.
They had a flavour reminiscent
Of baked Italian clay!

We've vacancies to fill yet,
There might be room for you,
Just come on any Monday
From eleven o'clock 'til two!

Keith Allison

COMPARING NOTES

'A single red rose for love's all I crave –
I'll get strawberry bath foam again!'
'I wish that they'd show a bit more romance
But that's too much to expect from mere men.'

'But yours tries so hard to show style and flair.
Your foot spa's a gift from the heart.'
'If you want it, it's yours, with great pleasure,' she said
'I'm not keen on a bath when it farts!'

'Champagne and roses for Valentine's Day!
Your husband's so romantic,' we sighed.
'But champagne for breakfast's not good for my diet!
Still at least I can say that he tried.'

I hear their chatter, think back through the years
With the man I decided to wed -
'Chocolates are fattening and flowers soon die
And wine? Well, we both prefer red!'

He doesn't buy presents, doesn't know what to get,
He'd rather I did the shopping instead.
No champagne or chocolate for Valentine's Day -
But I always get breakfast in bed.

Ruth Cargill

DO YOU KNOW YOUR ANGELS?

I ignored your prophecy of relief,
I do know the Jesus Christ belief,
Meanwhile you do speak of mystery,
I do know Jesus Christ's history.

Let's listen to angels' voices echo,
'Do not into the darkness go,'
That's the magic beauty of mystery,
And mystery of life's history.

I had drunk angels' divine water,
Listened to angels in divine crater;
I'd started to sing majestic melody,
Oh, out of my unique memory.

As voices started they lulled my soul to sleep,
Nowhere is that idea so deep;
Then I come back down to Earth again,
With the sun, the sand, the wind and rain.

There I saw a wondrous sight,
So clearly, floating clouds with light,
Mother Earth was covered by moon bright,
Oh, it out to be the brightest might.

Mystery stretched endlessly to sky,
Oh, until we get the wings to fly.
Angels have no doubts of Heaven and sin,
Or God's faith and justice within.

Milan Trubarac

MY MAMMY

I'm ten years old and I'm fed up and I'm going to tell you why,
'Cause every night Ma yells at me until I yawn and sigh,
'Wash your face, you dirty scamp, and scrub behind your ears
And get that muck off round your neck or I'll make you shed
                                                some tears.'
In I go to a cold bathroom and give myself a lick,
I want to see the telly, so my wash is double quick.
I'm doing fine 'til in she stamps and takes one look at me,
'You half-washed little chimney sweep - you're as black as coal
                                                can be.'
My poor wee head is tightly gripped between two big hands o' steel
I'm rushed o'er to the basin and I begin to squeal.
'Dad, come quick - she's drownin' me, she's comittin' a ruddy sin
My eyes are blinded wi' the soap and she's rubbin' off my skin.'
'Be quiet, you football addict, or you won't get any tea.
Unless this dirt comes off you, I'll steep you in DDT.'
When I'm looking like a lobster, she gives a great big smile,
'Now brush your teeth and comb your hair and sit by the fire awhile.
And the next time you play football in a field that's muddy with rain,
Make sure you play away from home, 'cause you're driving me insane.'
When I go to bed I lie awake and dream
Of scoring goals for England in a top division team.
Oh just you wait, Mammy, 'til I grow up and I become a man.
I'll be famous, I'll win cups and you'll be my biggest fan.

Janet Petchey

BUTTERFLY

Flutter by butterfly tapping on my window
Peeping through the glass outside trying to say hello
Showing me your pretty colours in a brilliant show
Before you spiral to the ground and the flowers below.

Flutter by butterfly I espy you at each flower
Shaking off the morning dew in a sparkling shower
Displaying your skill and beauty and your frail power
Beating your thin wings so hard as you bend each swaying tower.

Flutter by butterfly you've had a busy day
The sun is going down now and you've overspent your stay
Soon it will be dark outside and this I to you say
It's time for you to fly back home and flap your weary way.

Keith B Osborne

THE LONG NIGHT

It was just another day of many chores that all got done,
A decent meal or two, some bingo, again with nothing won,
An evening by the fire with my head stuck in a book,
Until my eyes no longer saw, however much I'd look.

I undressed in a sort of daze and crawled into my bed,
I revelled in its softness, the pillows soothed my head,
I closed my eyes and longed for sleep to while away the night,
Until the chirping of the sparrows would herald dawn's first light.

Whilst all my body craved for sleep, my brain was wide awake,
I tossed and turned, my limbs a-twitch, my tummy all a-quake,
My brain went back to all my moves from morning until night,
I went over all I'd done that day and wondered, was I right?

I listened to its ticking as the clock crawled through the night,
I plotted and I planned and I put the world to right,
I sent up a little prayer that almost made me weep,
'Oh God, if you're listening, *please* let me go to sleep.'

The hours passed, but oh, so slow, they scarcely seemed to go,
I watched the window endlessly to witness dawn's first glow,
It came at last, the night was gone, a new day almost here,
And as I watched, my eyelids drooped, and sleep was oh, so near.

I lay relaxed, my twitches gone, and settled down to sleep,
I knew that if I shut my eyes, I'd be gone without a peep,
I could feel that lovely drifting as my brain gave up the fight,
Then the ruddy alarm clock shrilled its goodbye to the night!

G M Baker

PIGS WITH A TASTE OF GALLIC

Many's the time I've heard them say
That pigs are not as grand today -
Noisier when they eat their food,
Gulping the swill-which is most rude,
Gobbling everything up so fast
That genteel creatures are aghast.
For when pigs dine they quite forget
Good manners and true etiquette.

Time was when porkers were polite,
Sitting at table as of right,
Folding napkins as they'd been taught
And using them just as they ought.
They never chewed with undue haste
But nibbled to enjoy the taste.
Only gourmet dishes were served
Because that is what these pigs deserved.

One Gallic chef, Antoine by name,
Was expert at the cooking game.
He planned each course and did it well
To please his porcine clientele.
Then all was style and elegance -
Nothing was ever left to chance.
The cutlery and china were
Always very superior.

The linen was the very best,
Embroidered with a snouted crest.
Each pig was then a bon viveur
And evening dress was de rigeur.
The boars, in smart tuxedo suits,
Drank French champagne from crystal flutes.
Sadly, those days have long passed by,
Now laissez-faire rules in the sty.

Celia G Thomas

WHIMSICALLY WEIRD

It was a hot summer's day,
        Snow was on the ground
The freshly made toffee pudding
        Was nowhere to be found,
Father Christmas was sleeping
        In his favourite chair
I heard a knock at the door,
        But nobody was there.

The wind was blowing backwards
        For everyone to see,
The gingerbread house was empty,
        Except for you and me.
A clown was in the corner
        Sobbing out his heart
The race was already over,
        Because it failed to start.

Black crow was in the pear tree
        Singing loud and sweet,
An elephant was out strolling
        With slippers on her feet.
A scarecrow was softly dancing
        In a field of maize,
An Eskimo thought of sunbathing
        In the wintry haze.

Three mice were playing poker
        With the farmyard cat,
The politician made news headlines
        Saying this was that.
Four painted gnomes were escaping
        Under the garden wall,
Several poets were in conversation,
        Saying nothing at all.

George S Johnstone

SORRY I DIDN'T MEAN TO - IT WAS AN ACCIDENT
(Dedicated to Benjamin and Nathan)

Sorry I locked you outside Mummy,
Didn't you think it was hilariously funny?

Mum, the telly won't come on,
Where did this juice all come from?
Sparks flying, juice running down the back of the telly,
At least it wasn't anything smelly.

Bubbles galore around the patio door,
Washing up liquid squirted all over the floor.
I know, let's wash it away with the watering can,
We could get more bubbles by using the fan.

Grandad's prize apples growing on the apple tree,
Look Grandad, we can have these for tea,
One for you and one for me.

Look Dad, I have locked myself in the car,
Don't worry, I won't go far.
I have the keys,
Go on Daddy, say 'Pretty please.'

Louise King

UNTITLED

Please don't think that I am flighty
But I wish your pyjamas were next to my nightie
Now don't get excited, and keep a cool head,
I mean on the clothes line and not in the bed.

Brenda Hill

THE SCHOOL RUN

It's .35
The alarm hasn't gone off,
The kids aren't dressed.
Uniforms in a heap on the floor.
Why aren't you dressed yet?
But Mum!

Mum can we have breakfast?
We haven't got time.
But Mum!
But Mum I am hungry.
So am I, but let's get dressed.
But Mum!

Running down the street,
Kid with toast in hand.
But Mum!
Mum wait for me.
Come on. It's late!
You're going to be late!

But Mum! Don't 'Mum' me!
School's in sight
But Mum!
What?
It's Saturday!

Sharron Rushton

My Holiday In Spain

Dear Lord, I'm going on holiday to Spain again.
I know I have asked you this again and again.
Get me there all safe and sound
And make the Euros good to our pound.
Give me grace to look my best,
Not walk about in a sleeveless vest!
I won't go topless on the sea shore
Because at my age, more means more.
Deliver me from the ticket touts
And keep me safe from lager louts.
Save us from the holiday 'reps'
Ask a question and the answer's, 'Yep.'
I know I am old but may I be bold
And ask you please to give me a hug
And keep me safe from the Benidorm bug.
I don't want to spend the holiday on the toilet seat,
So please bless everything that I shall eat.
And deliver me from the shopping spree,
Filling up my cases with 'duty free'
And round the markets please take heed,
Buying a load of rubbish that I don't need.
And when it's time and my holiday is done
And I'm sick to death of sand and sun
Get me home all safe and well.
Where to next? Who can tell?
Thank you Lord, I'll talk to you again,
Before my next holiday out there in Spain.

Ennis

LOST AND FOUND

We went into a cafe to get out of the rain -
What a start to a holiday - it seemed such a shame.
My husband went to the counter, to order a meal,
I took off my damp coat and felt more at ease.

The meal's a long time coming, I thought as I looked around,
But where had my husband gone? He was nowhere to be found.
The staff went and searched the loos, but all to no avail,
Then the door opened and to my joy he appeared again.

The relief on his face when he saw me
Showed he *still* loved me, after 33 years,
Then he grumbled that I'd taken off my coat -
And he thought I had disappeared.

Now I have to give him a warning
If I'm about to disrobe,
So he knows what I'm wearing
When I wander off alone.

Laura Harris

AYE AYE CAPTAIN

The old sea dog stood on the barrel and pail.
His belly was large, and his eye on the sail.
The captain's hat with bright yellow-gold braid
Was on his head as he stood on parade.
A cry rings out from a sailor below,
There's a monster! There's a monster!
It's coming up from the deep.
I'm being squeezed hard, I'll soon fall asleep.
How big is this monster?
Asked the captain with glee.
Fetch me a portion to have for my tea.
Aye, aye, Captain, said sailors all,
Then went down below to even the score.
So frightful the sight that they beheld,
The great creature lashed out;
More brave men were felled.
It's big! said one as big as a tree.
Oh no! Oh no! It's now after me!
The captain gave a disdainful look.
Who'll sail the ship if my sailors are took?
You boy . . . are you courageous enough?
I, Captain, I . . ? You go and get stuffed!
So the big man with his cat-o-nine tails,
Went down to assist and show he was bold;
Or so it is told.
For the only one left was the young cabin boy
To sail the ship, the ship Ahoy,
With a hold full of booze, the drunken swine!
Like the others . . . had his fill
On the rum and the wine.

Ronald D Lush

KIDS

A generation from my youth
The world has changed, that is the truth
Computers, mobiles, DVDs
New toys to click, eyes, ears to please.

My games were: skipping, marbles and hopscotch,
Today the entertainment's up a notch.
Less gross, more fine, let fingers play
Leave legs alone, they've had their day.

The world is fast, there is no time
So quickly eat and stay 'on line.'
The music's loud, 'twas ever so
But now the rhythm's all techno.

When I was young the family ate
As one with home-cooked food on every plate
Around the table, ideas flew
Our theories changing as we grew.

Today, to cook takes far too long
The mothers work, fathers have gone
A TV dinner makes more sense
Sitting and talking makes one tense.

The young today are very free
They drink, they smoke, 'club' endlessly.
They take their drugs to dance all night
Forget tomorrow, that's their plight.

They do what we did, that is true
'Under the sun, there's nothing new'
But we were older when we tried
The drugs, the booze and when we lied.

Today they try 'it' very young
What more to say, what's come is come!

Ruth Chignell-Stapleton

TEENAGE BOYS

Do you have teenage boys?
All grown up, no more toys
Some days, they are sweetness and light
Others, all they do is fight

'Have you done your homework?' I say
The reply, as always, 'Don't have any today!'
Occasional letters from the school
It appears my angel has broken another rule

Friends troop in across my door
Taking no notice of my just-cleaned floor
I shriek loudly, 'Leave trainers outside!'
My house no more is my joy and pride

How do six strapping lads fit in?
My son's bedroom is quite slim
Is that really music they're listening to?
Oh no! Four more are here, form a queue

It's eight o'clock, will you get up please
Leave your brother alone, don't tease
Your tie is wherever you left it, my son
Hurry up, or you'll have to sprint and run.

Why are your trousers flying at half-mast?
Please stop growing, how long can this last?
A new pair of trainers, 'What, already!' I say
You're still at school, so guess who pays

A part time job, on a Saturday maybe?
'Not yet Mum, my friends I won't see.'
'Think of the money you could earn'
He's gone, not listening, will I ever learn?

It's ten o'clock, where can he be?
He went out straight after tea
A message comes through on my phone,
'Please pick me up Mum, I'm tired and alone.'

After showering and cleaning his teeth
It's been a good day, not much grief!
He comes down to say goodnight
This angel in my life, he is my light.

Julie Livett

FOOD

I would love a tasty burger
With a slice of Cheddar cheese,
Lots of deep-fried onions
And tomato ketchup please.

I would love a plate of chips
And a battered piece of fish,
Covered with salt and vinegar,
Please grant this simple wish.

I would love a deep pan pizza
Ham and pineapple is the best
With a few slices of garlic bread
But I'd pass no kissing test!

I would love some sweet and sour pork
With special egg-fried rice
Followed by apple fritters,
I could eat the whole lot twice.

I would live a king prawn curry,
But please not so very hot
A long, cool beer as well
To help me eat the lot.

I'm feeling very hungry
What shall I have to eat?
The choice is enormous
As I walk down the high street.

Paul Duddles

LAST WILL AND TESTAMENT

Uncle Harry made a will
And yet there was dissension.
Thirty people dressed in black
Kept eyes upon the antique cat
That stood upon the window sill.

Other items of great worth
Created much contention.
Nephew wanted all the china,
Aunt said silver was much finer
And the brass upon the hearth.

The lawyer seated at the desk
Coughed to gain attention.
He said the boy who dug the plots
Cleaned the windows, washed the pots
Was willed the lot by Uncle's last bequest.

Muriel Reed

HELIANTHUS ANNUUS

The sunflower is a strange invention
Thought up by divine intention.
Nothing changes its decision
To grow and grow despite derision.
Is it simply to let it see
The shocking acts of you and me,
Or is there some other purpose?
Perhaps it's searching for the circus!

Betty Nevell

VACATION

'Enjoy yourself' - still rings in my ears,
And, 'Don't forget our souvenirs!'
The time has come for another charade,
With walks along the promenade.

This year I'm going to stake my all,
To get me a man, be he old, fat or bald.
I'm tired of wishing and living alone,
I'm determined to find a man of my own.

I bought me some hot pants and things you see through
Then, as a 'permissive' I'll make my debut.
I'll even consider a daring affair,
For last week I discovered my first grey hair.

I've bought a blonde wig to help me untwirl,
Cos nobody loves an old fashioned girl.
I'm treating this 'vac' as my last crusade
To save me from being a crusty old maid!

Milly Hatcher

Humour

This duchess, a lady of fashion,
My word she had plenty of passion,
As she jumped into bed with her lover, she said,
'Thank goodness it's not on ration.'

G Nicklin

I BOUGHT A BOOK

I bought a book in Book World
It was packed with sound advice
On how to be more confident
Successful, bright and wise

They said if you screamed
Very loudly you would let off steam
But then somebody called an ambulance
And I was carried away in a team

They promised a smile would lift the day
So I smiled at everyone as I went on my way
Hey, what are you laughing at? What is so funny?
Is this the result of my being sunny?

Body image is vital, the experts all say
So start working on it this very day
Look into the mirror, blow it a kiss
Act young and beautiful, don't I wish

Never say 'yes' when you mean 'no'
Wear a pink jumper when you feel low
They advised on a spot of exercise
Swimming, yoga, running on the spot
When I tried the yoga, it tied me in a knot

You are what you eat, good food is essential
So I cooked up the cabbage, sprouts and the lentils
Inside the cake shop my absence is keen
And now I am rather a nice shade of green.

Patricia Mullins

Principal Fear

There once was a fellow named Jasper,
At school he was thought a disaster:
His trousers were sullied,
He was constantly bullied,
And he was the ruddy headmaster.

Nigel Stanley

THE DOCTOR'S SURGERY

'Doctor, Doctor, what have I got?
A big, red spot is on my bot.'
'That's all right, nothing to fear,
It's because you drink too much beer.'
'How can beer make a spot?'
What a lot of tommyrot!
But - at the bar I sat a lot,
Must be how I got the spot.
The moral of this story is
When you next have a glass of beer,
Bottoms up, and stand up for the cheer.

Pearl Stebbings

WISH YOU WERE HERE

The sun is shining in Malta, the sea is a glorious blue,
The flowers along the cliff walk dazzle us with their hue.
Our apartment is clean and cheerful, our balcony looks out to sea,
We can watch the yachts in the harbour and fishing trips are free.
We caught numerous fish for breakfast, like whiting and mackerel
                                                                 so fresh,
The chef made it all look so easy, and the children just love the
                                                                  bright crèche.
The private pool in the courtyard is a haven of peace and rest,
Where we spend our day in seclusion and as a family we vote it
                                                                    the best.
You would love the flowers and the fishing, the birds that we see
                                                                  as we sail,
We hope to be back in a fortnight and we are sending a card in the mail!

Norma Rudge

ODE TO NAOMI

My kid is really quite a pup -
She surely knows which end is up!
She plays piano, sings and - oh
I quite forgot to let you know -
She's good at English and Religious Ed.,
(Her maths is better left unsaid!)

This great all-rounder smiles a lot,
But when she's sad, she's not so hot;
And when her temper is quite lost
It's me that has to pay the cost!
In coming days there'll be more stressing.
She'll drive me mad - and I'm not messing!

But all in all she's fine and dandy,
(And the Child Allowance comes in handy!)

Becky Garrett

SUPERGIRL'S CAT

Supergirl's cat is no normal moggy,
She's as grey as can be, like a night that's foggy!
With X-ray eyes to see through the walls,
And she balances so that she never falls.

Supergirl's cat is better by far
Than Superman's strength and Batman's car.
She uses her tail to unpick locks,
Has a nose like a dog and ears like a fox.

But when Supergirl's cat is done for the day,
After all the criminals are taken away
She loves to be petted, just like a dog
By Supergirl. Oh, and her real name is Mog!

Peter Coulter (13)

FRIDAY NIGHT

There the three of us stood
All misunderstood
A pint in our hand as drunk as ever
Friday night, the three men together

Brian said, 'I didn't text the wife when she was away,
I tried, but the words went astray.
She hugged me and kissed me, then threw a wobbly,
Why didn't you text me, don't you love me?

John said, 'Mine stays at home and watches TV,
She won't work at all, she wants to be free.
She walked the dogs round and round the field.
Then said *Why don't you walk them if that's how you feel?*

They both looked at me for an explanation
I choked on my beer in an exasperation
'Don't ask me why women are mental,
But I think their hormones are instrumental.'

The women were close by round another table,
Discussing us men as only they are able.
Lynn said, 'Brian didn't text me when I was away.
I blame the Word Cup. What do you say?'

Ann said, 'I can't go to work at all,
I'd sooner stay at home and have a ball.
I've walked the dogs round the field today,
It's more than enough with my brittle bones, what do you say?'

They looked at my wife with an expectant glee
They longed for a nod to say she'd agree,
But she smiled and laughed to their utter dismay,
Finished her drink and walked away.

John Foster

BRINY WHITING
(Or Whitebait, I'll show you some Winkles)

Davy Jones, his locker full, sat astride a cannon.
What plagued his mind was, could he find a Plaice to put a man in?
Thi-Sole 'ere, or Dover there,
He Dab soon wouldn't care.
Then he Smelt a Brill idea!
'Eel Jelly well Kipper Perch warm
With Salmon his Dogfish.'
'E's only a Shrimp though he has got Mussels,
Said Clamant Rockfish.
'Bream on!'
'No Cod,' said Davy,
'Don't be a Sprat; he was in the navy.'
'Crabsticks in my Mullet,' said Jones,
'And Turbot makes too many bones.'
'Don't Carp,' said Clam, who was hard of Herring,
'I've been to see Halibut, she wasn't stirring.'
'Now Mackerel effort,' said Davy, 'and hear what I say.
Oh Cockles and Scallops, he's gone away!'
So Davy Jones, his 'ed all Hakey, a Prawn his forty-pounder
Thought it Trout but he never Flounders
Bass to put the old Sardine.
(Ask me the old Pilchard wants cannin'.)
Not averse to plannin'.

Philip Beverley

UNTITLED

The noise of the crowd came over wall
As with one voice they shouted 'Goal!'
'United, United,' the chanting swelled as
If by a force nine gale impelled.
The listener waited for the din to die down,
Hoping the next goal would be for the Town.
He had been too late to get into the ground,
Now like a caged animal he paced round and round.
A whistle shrilled out and the crowd fell quiet,
Next moment he heard a noise like a riot.
What was it? A penalty? Someone sent off?
He ran to the turnstile to hear the speaker,
The excitement, he found, was caused by a streaker.

Marjorie Grant

ONE MONDAY MORNING

There goes the alarm, jump out of bed.
Take it easy, I've banged my head!
Stand up straight, I've lost the knack.
Too much haste, I've strained my back!

Collect my clothes from off the floor . . .
Rushing around, walk into the door!
Quickly to the bathroom go -
Hurriedly wash the bits that show!

Clean my teeth and comb my hair,
No one said this life was fair.
I'm late for work, why should I worry?
I make mistakes whenever I hurry.

Spill my coffee and burn the toast.
All of these things I hate the most.
To tell the truth it's such a pain . . .
I think I'll go back to bed again!

But no - I'm going off to work -
I know my duty, I cannot shirk.
You know the way that all things are.
Now I can't start the blessed car!

It starts at last, and here I am . . .
Stuck in an awful traffic jam!
I reach the lights and they turn red,
I really wish I'd stayed in bed!

I reach the car park, it could be worse,
I just can't get the car in reverse!
I crunch and grind the gears together,
Who said, 'Better late than never'?

The lift's out of order, so up I climb,
Flight after flight - 'What is the time?'
I reach my door in a breathless state,
What reason can I give for being so late?

Into the office I walk with care,
To discover that I'm the only one there.
No one's about to hear what I say . . .
Because today is - *a bank holiday!*

Maureen Ayling

IF PIGS COULD FLY

If pigs could fly
We'd have a job
Just getting all our bacon.
Maybe we would have a plate
Where rashers are forsaken.
The eggs sit there in loneliness
Even sausages aren't on.
If pigs could fly
What would there be?
... A breakfast almost gone!

Barry Clist

A MUSICAL MYSTERY

Can you understand opera?
I just can't get the hang.
I saw one where a man got stabbed;
He didn't die - he sang!

Mozart wrote a lot of them,
Wagner and Verdi too;
Then later still there's Alban Berg,
Who wrote one called 'Lulu.'

Lulu is a Scottish lass,
A pop star grand is she;
So how come she's an opera?
Ah, that's the mystery!

Roger Williams

MENIERE'S DISEASE

My head is full of titanic bees
At least that's how they sound
And when the bees grow quiet
The silence is profound.
But alas,
That state of affairs never lasts long
Because a giant bell starts to peel
Its dissonance drives me crazy
And the nausea is an ordeal . . .
And then,
I do my drunken sailor act
And stagger hither and thither
Just as it seems things can't get worse,
My whole being starts to quiver.
Which results
In my going base over apex
Then the only sensible thing to do
Is to take my wobbly body off
To bed for an hour or two.
There's more
Of cacophony than symphony
Within my spinning head,
My doctor says, I'll find some peace
If I go deaf . . . or when I'm dead!

V M McKinley

THREE'S A CROWD

When the baby was brought for inspection
Father threw off his mood of dejection;
He welcomed the mite
With pride and delight -
Till he heard two more claimed his protection!

Dorothy Elthorne-Jones

NOT TOO SURE

Life begins at 40, some folks say
Beware, don't get too excited and carried away
Things always happen that bring some doubt.
Times have to change, that's what life is all about.
In the bathroom for instance, when you do your hair
You reach for the Silvikrin, there's some grey showing there.
That last suit you bought, oh dear, the trousers are tight,
Memories of being slim, you grimace and say, 'Right,
I'll cut out the wine, the sugar, the sweets,
I'll exercise regularly, no more MacDonald's treats.
I'll eat plenty of salads and in my lunch break,
I'll don a tracksuit and not make the mistake
Like when I was a baker, and could not resist
The custard slices, the doughnuts, with jam oozing out
                                      in a beautiful twist.'
40 years on looking back and remember
The school days and your mum, so loving and tender.
When it rained, if you had to play football, your mum sent a note
Can you remember the words that your mum always wrote?
You dreaded the sports master shouting, getting ready to throw it.
'My Freddie must not get wet,' and all the school knew it.
40 years on, shorter in wind as in memory long,
Is it time to think twice about training for that half-marathon?
There's those jobs the missus requested, that I keep putting off,
Whatever I do, she and the kids giggle and scoff.
How I regret not listening to my woodwork master,
Oh dear, I wish I could plaster.
In the DIY shop I stop and have to think.
Colours confuse me, I can't tell the difference between orange and pink.
But whatever folks say, there is not any telling
What height I might achieve with these goods I am selling.
I could be the top rep at the end of the year
And the missus will say, 'Never mind, Dear.

We don't mind if you are plump and wobble a bit,
If you have had a hard day, on your knee I will sit

With the kids to tell you, we love you and just want to say,
You are our own special hubby and daddy.
Many happy returns of the day.'

Fred Norgrove

ABOUT ME

Before my bedroom mirror,
Many hours I have spent,
And every time I look in it
I see what Darwin meant.

My many cousins at the zoo
Are very plain to see,
And every time you look at one
It might as well be me!

Pleione Tooley

THE PRINCE AND THE CORGI

One of the corgis said to the prince,
'Could you make me a poultice of mince,
With gravy and onion
To put on my bunion?
The pain is making me wince.'

The prince said, 'I'm sorry, I can't;
You see, you are just not a plant.
Now a pink busy lizzie
Would have me quite busy;
But your wish, I just cannot grant.'

'Look you, boyo!' the corgi growled through is jaw,
'Don't you know it's against the law
To leave a dog in a mess
And cause it distress,
When it can barely stand up on its paw?'

'Look, I'll tell you what I will do,
As a special concession to you.
I'll ring up old Rolf
To come in from his golf
And play you his didgeridoo.'

'And a fat lot of good that will be
When I'm in pain up to my knee!
You could at least call a vet
To your mother's sick pet;
After all, you can afford the fee.'

The vet came and had to convince
The royal stuffed shirt of a prince,
That the cure for a bunion
Is gravy with onion,
Mixed in with a spoonful of mince!

Kathy Rawstron

BOYS WILL BE BOYS

Said the fairy to Wee Willie Winkie,
'What say, shall we go to the ball?'
So dressed in their best
From their long johns to vest,
They made for the old village hall.

Now the fairy was gorgeous and pretty,
In her tinsel and frilly pink dress.
With her wand and her crown,
She brought the house down,
All except for the hairs on her chest.

And Wee Willie Winkie looked sweet, dears,
In his nightie and bobbles so gay,
With his candle aglow,
He quite stole the show,
Had his tummy not got in the way.

She was really the most hairy fairy,
With her baggy long johns hanging low,
But with corpulent Wee Willie Winkie,
The fancy dress ball was all go!

Joan Hammond

Diddle, Diddle, Dumpling

Diddle, diddle, dumpling, my pal John,
Went off to work with no clothes on.
First he was hot
And then he was cold,
And then was arrested
For being so bold.

E M Higgins

GREENS

I did so wish that a liking for greens
And suchlike food was within my means,
To savour, munch and masticate,
When piled in heaps upon my plate.

My teacher told me every day
There's only one method, only one way.
If you want to be happy, hearty and hale,
One must eat one's greens as a cow chews kale.

'Twas then I had a terrible fright
And awoke with a start in the dead of the night.
What a silly idea to get in my head,
How a great Brussels sprout chased me right round the bed.

But I conquered my fears and strove with a will,
And always was happy and never was ill.
And when folks admired me, ah, 'twas then I could say,
Cos I ate all my greens up, each every day.

G F Watts

EASY DOES IT

What is the good of being prescribed medication
When folk cannot open the lids?
It is done for safety as we all know
Protection for 'the kids.'
Strangely enough if we live alone
We are really up the creek
Waiting for someone to come and call
It could take up to a week.
There is no problem at all when the grandchildren come
They know exactly what to do
They take the bottle in their deft little hands
They press and then they unscrew.
'We can do it! We can do it, Gran!
No need to wait for someone to call,
A lady or a man.'
When one is old with arthritic hands
It makes one feel so silly
When we cannot open our bottle of pills
But is done by grandson, Billy.

E A Evans

NIGHT-TIME RAMBLINGS

Before modern sanitation, no bathroom had old Fred,
To answer calls of nature, he used an outside shed.
One night he felt an urgent call and quickly crossed the floor,
In his haste and by mistake, he opened the wrong door.

In the cupboard there he stood, shelves were stacked with shopping,
He hummed a tune as the flow showed no sign of stopping.
In the kitchen sat his wife, she called, 'Where are you dear?
I fear the weather is to change, is it rain I hear?'

'The night is dark,' replied old Fred, 'no stars are in the sky,'
As he stood he let out a most contented sigh,
Then a thought occurred to him, it puzzled poor old Fred,
In the darkness of the night, he got a smell of bread.

Alister H Thompson

NANNY AND HAZEL

Nanny and Hazel are sisters,
They make me laugh and say rude things,
'I'll pull your legs off and
Put them in the bin.
I'll tear you limb from limb,
Take every single hair out, one by one,
And prick you with a pin,
and then . . .

Throw tablet boxes at you,
And push you out the door.
Singing, 'Deck The Halls With Boughs Of Holly,'
And make you scream, *'No more!'*
I'll put a spider in your duvet,
Watch you squirm and squeal, *'Heyyyy!''*

Nanny and Hazel are born witches,
Currently known as Barbara and Maureen.
Pure evil, they plot against each other.
They could end up on Big Brother.
Once they start, they never stop,
Until each other's heads go *pop!*
And then . . . (will this ever end?)

Adam Teeling

THE OUTSIZE FAMILY

There was an old woman who lived in a shoe
But what a load of rubbish saying she didn't know what to do.
She never took precautions, and she knew about the pill,
She was after kids' allowances, with us to foot the bill.
They never mention Superdad, the lazy, idle jerk,
He was on the dole because of all his nightly work.
They all went on the housing list to try and find a place,
With four and twenty bedrooms, and lots and lots of space.
The poor old local council, really had the hump,
Until they found this giant's shoe on a nearby rubbish dump.
So they set about conversion - polished up this shoe,
Filled it up with rooms and stairs, and a great big outside loo.
A big, long, twenty seater, a really super job
And supplied a ton of toilet rolls to accommodate this mob.
Thus was solved the problem of this outsize family,
And the children's fairy story, really came to be.

John Townend

AGE

Why does every birthday reinforce the law of gravity?
And hair, receding from the head, now grow from every cavity?
It's nature's most vindictive, reprehensible depravity;
Experience could pave the way for comfort, ease and fun.

But every single working part gets harder to maintain;
Now, where there once was colour, only lighter shades remain,
And any small abuses bring ten times their weight in pain
As any careless damage now can never be undone.

But if I had the chance to be a teenager once more
With the same lack of perspective, or knowledge, as before
I'd only want to do it if I knew I could be sure
I could return when hope's succumb to reason had begun.

Gaynor Florence Perry

THE ECO WARRIOR

Dear old Aunt Matilda
Was an eco friendly lass.
She collected all her paper, tin-foil,
And her coloured glass.

She loved her garden dearly
And she kept a compost heap,
And all the slugs and creepy things
Chewed at the stuff like sheep!

The worms did all the dirty work
And lived in rotting veg.
Small grey trundling woodlice
Chewed cuttings on the edge.

Aunt turned the heap a few times
As nature took her hold,
And out of all the rubbish came
Fine compost, earthy gold!

One day aunt died while gardening.
Getting wet in April showers.
She had a cardboard coffin,
Painted with coloured flowers.

Now sweet Matilda's ashes
On compost can be found.
An eco-warrior of the past,
To fertilise the ground.

All the little creatures
Dining on the compost heap
Are sharing it with Auntie
While she is fast asleep!

Linda A Knight

THE TAX MAN

April brings the tax man
Knocking at my door,
Sends me his 'assessment'
Chills me to the core.
All year long I work hard
Doing what I can,
Then comes retribution
From this evil man.
Still I know deep down that
I've just got to pay,
Doesn't make it easy
Come the fateful day.

Daniel Jack

BRAY

There was a young girl from Bray
who was taught never to go the whole way.
Imagine her surprise when she found,
after a time, that her belly went round
regretting the time she didn't say nay.

Alan Seaward

THE TRUCE

There was a boy called Gus
Who always missed the bus.
'Five minutes more, Mum,' he would plea,
'I'll be there first, you wait and see.'

'It is no use,' his mother cried,
'He'll get his own - baked, boiled or fried.
I've had enough of Gus,' and off she went with no more fuss.
To Gran's she went, no doubt for tea.
A chat; some sympathy for me.

But Gran's blue eyes were stern and grim,
'You'll lose him, like you did your Jim.
Go right back there, don't stand and stare,
Just hit and miss, with a great, big kiss.'
She gathered speed.
There was no need to remember. The solemn vow.
Love and cherish, shall not perish.
Oh Gus, forgive me now.
And thereon the table was a rose, pink, pale, like Gus's nose.
We laughed and laughed.
I felt so daft as we kissed.

My heart was light, as Gus took flight.
He always missed the bus.

Hilda Ellis

THOSE AUSTRIAN BLINDS

Oh dear Jim,
I sympathise,
All those Austrian blinds
Before your eyes.
Frills and ruffles,
Not really you,
So feminine, pink and cream,
Why didn't your wife choose blue?
When Mary's
On the curtain track,
It does no good
To draw her back.
Oh no! This blind does not fit!
What a pain!
Take it back
To the shop again.
Now dear Jim,
Be patient, smile, do not frown,
And very soon you will see you have,
The smartest windows in the town.

Carol Ann Darling

THE CARER

Gwendolin, oh Gwendolin,
Your humour shows each day.
You make us laugh when you come in,
We love to hear you say,
'Good morning girls - now stop that din.
You're here to work, not play.'

Your Yorkshire frankness often shows,
But it is really kind.
You bear so many people's woes,
And calm their troubled minds.
Our home has 33 of them,
And only one of you.

But stressed and tired, no job's too small,
Love shows in all you do.
You've time to listen to them all,
And give the care they need from you.
You're there, they only have to call,
You calm the fears of one and all.

And when your daily work is done,
Your faithful car awaits
To whisk you home to man and dog,
So don't you dare be late.
Just when you think, 'All tasks complete,'
You find the blighters want to eat.

Betty Smyth

Daddy's Train Set

My daddy's got a train set,
He says it is for me,
But I never get a look in
When it comes out after tea.

My daddy's got a train set
With which I'd like to play,
But when he isn't in the house
He locks it all away.

My daddy's got a train set
That really can't be mine,
Because he uses it himself
In all of his spare time.

My daddy's got a train set
And I am really fed up,
'Cause I'll never get to play with it
Until my dad grows up!

Joyce Walker

WHERE ARE THE ROSES?

Midweek of June closes and where are the roses?
    There's hardly a bud in sight.
No butterflies flutter; only one supposes
    They're having a nice long night.
No moths haunt the darkness; and where is the cuckoo?
    She must have a cold in her head;
I haven't yet heard her, she doesn't say, 'Look you,
    My chick is the one you've fed.'

Oh shame on you, summer! I've sent for the plumber
    To deal with my waterlogged house.
The salads aren't growing, there's not enough showing
    To gladden the heart of a mouse.
The clouds keep on forming - where *is* global warming?
    It must have been lost in the post.
Outside it is sleeting, so turn up the heating,
    It's 13 degrees at the most.

But I know summer's coming to set the bees humming,
    Enthusiasts venture outdoors.
With strawberry teas, still, June, you may please -
    From Wimbledon rings our applause!
You have just one more chance your repute to enhance,
    O June of 2002;
Just turn on the sun before July's begun,
    And we still may speak kindly of you!

(But she didn't!)

Kathleen M Hatton

A Good Catch

A man was fishing in a lake beside a shady hedge,
Standing in his wading boots in the long green sedge,
He wasn't having much luck, in fact he hardly had a bite,
Feeling worried because he had promised fish for tea that night.
When the evening clouds rolled up, he worried all the more,
So he gathered up his tackle and went to the fishmonger's door,
'Have you any fish left over?' he said to the fishmonger who
                                                                              was his mate,
'I've been fishing all day long and I've still only got my bait,
I will feel such an idiot when I go home to the wife,
She will say I am no good to her. Can you save my life?'
The fishmonger picked him out some fish and put it in a sack,
Feeling happy with himself the man took his homeward track,
His wife was pleased, she was proud of what he said he had caught,
Of course only the fishmonger knew what he had really bought.
Making a fuss of him, gave him a kiss and passed him his slippers,
Opening up the sack she said, 'It's the first time I have seen
                                                         any freshwater kippers.'

Stan Gilbert

MONSTERMAN

There once lived a monster under a child's bed.
One day the monster spoke, and this is what he said.
'I'm sick of living under there,
There's lots of fluff and balls of hair!
I've had enough, I'm moving out,'
With that he slammed the door with a bang and a shout.
Now the child has a good night's sleep
Cos the monster's gone, and so has its cheek!

Louise Lee

MY KNIGHT

Good King Arthur became my knight
Saving me from many a plight
In my dreams he came to me
Stirred my heart and turned the key

Tall and handsome he was built
Enough to make a maiden wilt
Guinevere he'd left behind
Making sure he's hard to find

Adventures we did share each night
Many a villain put to flight
Through the forests we did ride
Excalibur always by his side

One glorious night he did come
But Merlin the wizard spoilt our fun
History we were writing anew
For Merlin that would never do

Arthur on his charger was sent
Far away to the land of Gwent
I was put to a dreamless sleep
Never more my knight to meet.

Hazel Mills

THE WEDDING

I was a guest at a wedding a fortnight ago,
My hat was so big it stole the show,
I slipped and caught at the table top,
The contents fell off, and the cake went flop.

The bride was in tears, the guests in a frenzy,
I never saw so much fuss by so many,
The waiters descended with buckets and mops,
The groom slipped and sat down in a puddle of soap.

By then it was a mass hysteria,
Among those present was the media,
The pressmen smiled and sent their cameras clicking,
They would report on this very different wedding.

I slipped off quietly as could be,
I thought it best to do this you see,
For they might have thought that I was jinxed,
The wicked genie in their midst.

Elizabeth Hiddleston

My Dilemma

A handsome young man, with an engaging grin,
Knocked on my door and asked to come in.
I checked his credentials and said okay,
Curious about what he wanted to say.
He thought I appeared a lady of sense,
Who budgeted well with my pounds and pence.
If I would sign on the dotted line,
Great wealth would shortly be mine.
His words were honeyed and he had me bemused,
I'd be an idiot if I refused.

I agreed to give his offer some thought
But in the end it all came to nought.
A second man called the very next day,
I invited him in to have his say.
So distinguished, debonair, he quite impressed
With his savoir faire.
He too promised to fill my coffers,
If only I would consider his offers.
I ask you, what's a girl to do
With two nice chaps coming to woo?
A difficult choice, alack and alas -
Scottish Power or British Gas!

Ivy Stewart

HILL WALKING ON MARS

Walking easy, walking easy,
leave the valley far below,
passing meadows green and golden,
aiming for the peaks of snow.

Breathing faster, breathing faster,
plagued by flies and droning bees,
steeper grows the path and stony,
problems now for hips and knees.

Pounding upwards, pounding upwards,
one of us now starts to curse,
now the way is getting tougher,
the others say it could be worse.

Sweating freely, sweating freely,
how far now before we stop?
I can't go on a minute longer,
must eat a Mars before I drop!

Alice Rawlinson

TICKLED PINK

Once when I was in the bath
my pet octopus made me laugh.
He told me a joke
and we both turned red.
Laughing hard as you do
when the joke amuses you.
The octopus did not stop to think
and finished covering me in ink.
With embarrassment the poor octopus
turned a pale shade of pink.
He decided to cool himself off
ran some water, then jumped into the sink.
Sitting there he was quite happy
and is a good little chappie.
But when taking an octopus out of the sink
mind you don't get squirted with ink.
Of a better friend I could not think
we are both tickled pink.

S Glover

MAKING THE BED

Trotting around, stripping the bed
Is jolly hard work it has to be said.
Cases for pillows, pulled off in a hurry
Sheets and valance add to the flurry
Now to be washed and out on the line -
Do hope the sun will continue to shine!
Later, when dry and smelling so sweet
(I hardly notice I've been rushed off my feet)
Ironed and folded, all smooth and pristine
There's nothing like bedding that smells fresh and clean
Then it's back to the bedroom to make up the bed
It's jolly hard work, it has to be said.
Corners are mitred, sheets smoothed quite flat
Sides neatly folded, ends tucked in pat.
From such strenuous work my back is bent double
Did ever a job cause quite so much trouble.

And for what?

When bedtime comes, I'll collapse in a heap
But dreams will elude me, I'll be too tired to sleep
Tossing and turning, the sheets all undone
Alas and alack, it's back to *square one!*

Joanna Pickett

Lippy Limerick

There was a young chef named Trevor
Whose cooking was light as a feather
One day he looked glum
So I pinched his bum
And that sent him off in a tether.

Joanne Wilcock

PIGS MIGHT FLY

Gather around now, children hurry,
Quickly run, jump and scurry.
For I am about to tell you the story,
About a pig in all its glory.
I hear you cry, 'By gum, what's new?'
But you did not see the view.
The pig was not on the ground,
In the sky was where it was found.
The facts are true that now I utter,
Because in the air the pig did flutter.

Well people flocked from all around
To see the pig above the ground.
Some came to simply observe,
While others caused the traffic to swerve.
The sheep in the next field were obviously jealous,
About the pig's attentions becoming zealous.
The cows too began to complain,
With deep scorn and disdain.
But the chickens did not seem to mind,
Although the feed became unkind.

You see the fame had gone to the farmer's head,
And rather than feeding the others instead,
He did not compromise the money coming in,
Resulting in the loss of din.
The other animals began to revolt,
It really was not all their fault,
Because with the talk of the flying pig,
The farmer's profits had grown too big.
As the reputation had spread far and wide,
So the price of bacon had multiplied!

Ruth Morris

ON FIRST LOOKING INTO PEOPLE'S HUMOUR
(With apologies to Keats)

Much have I travelled in the realms of fun,
And many varied kinds of laughter heard.
From tiny titter up to great guffaw,
Each sound of pleasure has its fitting word.

A cackle is the noise a hen might make
When tickled with a long and curling feather;
A giggle is what silly girlies do
When eyeing up the talent clothed in leather.

A snigger is the province of a lad
Who cracks a dirty joke for pals at school;
A chortle is majestic, nay, triumphant,
When Dad at last proves Boss Man was a fool.

A scream of laughter rends the air asunder
(It's not the nicest noise in my opinion)
A hoot is not just meant for sundry owls
But for punsters, witty folk and jester's minion.

I've counted up the terms in my synonymy -
Eleven entries worth a second look.
A reassuring sign of healthy sanity
Silent upon a peek in Roget's book.

D M Anderson

LIMERICK

A lovely young lady of Herm
Washed her hair out and gave it a perm,
Then posed without nightie
As Herm Aphrodite -
She still is serving her term!

Barrie Williams

LAUGHING LESLIE

Laughing Leslie laughed so loud
His laugh could be heard above the crowd
His laugh was of an extremely high pitch
He ended up with an awful stitch

The more he laughed, the more he cried
Enormous tears ran down his side
He laughed so much he began to choke
Until his laugh ended up as a croak
Which laughing Leslie found 'no joke!'

Christine Hardemon

HUSBAND'S NEW SHORTS

My husband, he is a really good sport
So when he announces
'I need some new shorts'
Wife and offspring, we nod and smile
For he's hardly a guru of fashion and style.

In choosing colour, he's laid back, cool
Blue or brown he'll select as a rule.
His girth gives him problems
Needs generous cut,
Space for his tummy, smooth on the butt.

Off he sallies, new shorts look good,
We smile and approve, as his loved ones should.
Do we give 'thumbs down' if they look awfully bad?
Why no, we smile sweetly
Remember he's Dad!

Pamela Carder

Cassius Clay

Who is this man called Clay?
A fighter he says in my day.
When doing the shuffle
He got in a scuffle
And was promptly knocked out by Will Hay.

E Gosney

THE JUMBLE SALE

Saturday come rain or gale, see us at the jumble sale,
Whether it be wet or fine, fighting to be first in line,
Clutching bags huge and capacious, on the hunt we are voracious
For the bargains piled on high.
Quick, the doors are open wide, hurry, hurry, get inside,
Jabbing elbows, prodding brollies, watch out for the shopping trolleys.
Hang on tight to what you're grasping, I'm exhausted, hot and gasping.

Guess it was all worth a try.
Old folks who are hardly mobile suddenly find they are agile
Gone are signs of *artheritis* as for bargains they all fight us.
Scrabbling underneath each trestle as they with each other wrestle,
Not a whimper, not a cry.
But come Monday at the clinic, 'Nurse, my back is something chronic.
Can I see the doctor please? Something's happened to my knees,
Can I have some pills and tonic?' But next week, turned supersonic
Once more fighting tooth and nail, there's another jumble sale!

S A Baker

My Friend Gillian

Gillian is a bag of bones
And one day she had bad pains,
They took her to the hospital
And said she had got rolling stones.

'Oh boy,' she said, 'I love that group,'
The doctor said, 'They are fab,'
Then the very next thing they saw
Was a man running round with a black bag?

They thought it was Doctor Jekyll,
But it might have been Doctor Hyde,
They said if you do not settle,
We shall have to have you inside.

Before her visitors came to see her,
They had to change, have a shave and a shower,
The poor little lonely soul
Had to wait for many an hour.

The ward was like bedlam,
Patients jumping out of their beds,
Man and bag peeped through the curtains
And said, 'Cheer up, you will soon be dead.'

The man with the black bag was her husband,
The doctor said, 'Sit down and be quiet,
We have got your wife in hand,
Everything's going to be all right.'

May Ward

THE RAZZLE DAZZLER

I'm Pansy Potter the chamber maid,
I work at the Razzle Hotel,
I clean the rooms, serve high tea,
And look after the guests as well.

It's not much money, the uniform's crummy,
You should see the things that I see;
I call all the couples, madam and sire,
I've got it up top you see.

If a man's on his own, and I think he is prone,
I'll give him a peck on the cheek,
It's always good for a quid or so,
And maybe he'll come back next week.

The best paying guests, the ones I love best,
Are the ones who carry full wallets,
I sit on their beds, flashing my legs,
Watching their eyes pop like comets.

If I fancy a guy, I don't charge a fee,
He gets his deserts for nothing,
If he only brings candy and then gets all randy,
I tell him he's asking for stuffin'.

The manager's cute, he's single to boot,
I think he fancies my chassis, he's got a dark skin,
Foreign I'd say, just like Aristotle Onassis.

Well I s'pose I must move, and start changing beds,
And make all the rooms nice and tidy.
Have a nice weekend, I'll do the same,
Today is pay day, it's Friday.

L Nokes

HUMOUR

The dear old, absent-minded professor
Was late in getting out of bed.
He entered the room for breakfast,
Kissed his egg,
Then tapped his wife on the head.

Mary Chadwick

WALLY WIMPOLE

Wally Wimpole went to town
And on his forehead wore a frown.
Wonder what the frown was for?
He'd lost the key to his front door.
Where could it be? old Wally wondered
And slowly as his temper thundered,
He tripped upon a pavement high
And bruised his leg and hurt his thigh.
Now off to hospital Wally went
Still frowning, bruised and bent
And lay there weeping for a while,
Until a nurse with such a smile
That Wally wondered, was his weeping
Really all that worth the while.
'Right then,' said nurse, 'off with your clothes.'
And Wally's warts and turned-up toes
Were such a funny sight to see,
Until they laughed hysterically.
The laughter grew till suddenly
A chinking sound, as if a key,
Had fallen to the cold stone floor
And Wally's key was lost no more.

John Wayre

The Black Cat

The cat fell into the bucket
As the man was mixing cement.
He threw the water on the mixing
And the cat turned out like a tent!

The man looked down in horror
As it tried to straighten out -
I wish it was tomorrow
With the cat just running about!

Get out the hosepipe, turn on the tap
Before the cement overlaps!
Let the water flow like torrential rain,
Then the cat will be meowing again!

Marie Barker

IN THE SUPERMARKET

With springy stride or tottery tread
Each goes to buy her daily bread.
Some know what they want, others with
A muddled head, through shopping aisles
Do tread, pushing trolleys slow ahead.

Handbag slung on doughty shoulder this
Thrusting throng could not seem bolder;
Fat bottom or skinny shin, angel face
Or devilish grin, on, on they go, on, on
Matchstick women in a throng.

But see a cripple's lame advance - don't
Stare or show a pitying glance - the path,
The way, is hard for them; your path, your
Way, is but a sham to their advance.

Now to the car park - to a shiny limo
Or rusty Ford, or just the bus?
Matchstick women home from limbo with
Shopping bags full to bust!

Michael Rowson

Bank Holiday

Dogs start to bark
And children shout
Strimmers and lawnmowers
Everyone's out
I go to the churchyard
For a ride on my bike
Even then there is no respite
The bell in the tower
Dongs a mournful note
I go to the river for a sail in my boat
The engine conks out, and my oar's afloat
So - back to my garden
Oh what a farce
As I sniff at the flowers
A wasp stings my a***
Now I begin to feel quite insane
Then suddenly it starts to rain
Being soaked to the skin doesn't bother me
Because it's peaceful now, you see.

Doris Lilian Critchley

GOD'S SPECIAL DAYS

Our vicar, he sent round a dish
It came back all loaded up with fish
How can I ever run this church
With a plate of chub, bream and perch?
Then a thought came in his head
Have a feast on fish and bread,
Send the verger to the petrol station
Get some bread for the congregation
Put a barbecue upon the altar
Cook the fish in the Holy water
Said everyone, now let's give praise
To God for giving us His special days.

Our vicar wanted to stop all sin
So he set up in the church a gym.
If God said you must not steal,
You can spend each night on the wheel.
Do not take my name in vain
Exercise till you hurt with pain.
You will have no God but me
A loss of your weight you'll see.
How our vicar found it strange
How the congregation did change.
One of God's most magic ways
To make this one of His special days.

Colin Allsop

Summer Fate

Roger Egg and Bill Spoon
had never met till the day of the race.
They came together in the hospital grounds
quite unexpectedly.
They raced together in ambulances,
hearts stopping, pace dropping,
pills popping, lightning flashed
as the van dashed,
but spoon flopped and egg dropped.
No prizes, just flower vases
and all to report was battles well fought.
The race was over,
they both lay on the clover,
tears and crashes now only ashes.

Vann Scytere

SPARKS

An electrician I've always wanted to be
Attended college daily, to learn mastery,
Blue wires, yellow, some brown and green
Only fault being they're all the same to me,
Reason being I'm colour blind you see.

After five years, I started up on my own
Rented myself an office, bought a mobile phone
First job was a nightmare, blew the roof off
Only used the live wires, instead of blue and earth.

Customer got quite irate, you're off to prison for that,
I can only see the sky now, it was once my flat.
I settled out of court, no point to argue toss,
My business empire, was soon running at a loss.

Ploughed more money into it, hoping upon hope
I would recover losses and not look such a dope.
Second job went better, until my mate had gone
Then the dreaded moment, I switched the electric on.

Crash, flash, bang, wallop! Another roof was gone
Ending up in court this time, I had to pay the bill
Judge warned me I must try to learn a new skill,
But now no one will employ me, and I don't know if I oughta
Forget about electric, and concentrate on water.

Grant Sulkin

THE SHOE SHOP GIRL

The shoe shop girl just smiled at me,
You want sandals? pouted she.
Sandals in the month of June?
You really are quite out of tune.

Fur boot stocks have just come through,
So buy some without more ado,
You'll be wanting them at Christmas next,
Please stop looking so perplexed.

Fleecy slippers, winter wear
When will the public come aware,
Are ordered six months in advance,
We do not leave these things to chance.

Summer sandals, paddling shoes,
Arrive at Christmas for you to choose
From a comprehensive range,
Madam, is that so very strange?

You fear your children's feet will grow,
I've heard it all before, you know;
So if you will pardon me,
It's time I had my cup of tea.

Although I say it half in jest,
I say I work on their behest,
Blame computer, office policy,
No one gets the best of me.

I'm going to get a raise in pay,
For the prompt and efficient way
I deal with problems every day,
The boss has got his eye on me, appreciates my loyalty.

Marian Voice Gifford

IT WAS A FUNNY THING

He laughed, she laughed, I laughed,
then everybody laughed
it was a funny thing
the tears ran down our faces
we made the rafters ring

Some roared, some cried
some wailed then sighed
and gasped for air to laugh anew
one soul passed care, fell off his chair
we were a merry crew.

Then suddenly it all went tame
to the room a silence came
were we spent, our feelings vent
laughed our last, the magic past

Then came a titter, then a twitter
we tried to stop in vain
but laughter is infectious
and we were off again
it was a funny thing.

Phil Aylward

THERE AND BACK

The fife and the fiddle
Were stuck in the middle
Of Ramsey, by the sea.
They couldn't get out
And started to shout
'Oh somebody, please help me!'

But there was a bus
Who heard their fuss
And whisked them away to Peru.
When it finally stopped
Off the bus they hopped
And said, 'Who the devil are you?'

As, in front of them
Was a man named Sven
Who thought they looked mighty odd.
Before they could ask
He gave them a flask
And introduced them to Todd.

'He will take you
Away from Peru
You don't even have to plea.'
And before they could say
'Have a nice day,'
They were back at Ramsey-on-Sea.

Camillia Zedan

THE BEST MEDICINE

I caught the bus and climbed to the top,
With babe in arms I was about to drop.
It was time for his feed
So I put him on breast
But he cried and refused and I said what I thought best.
'Drink up, drink up, or I'll go spare
And give it to the man sitting over there.'

Jo Taylor

GET TOGETHER IF YOU CAN

The old schoolgirls sat at the reunion table
Intent on gathering as much scandal as able
The first hurdle was recognising who was who
It's surprising what plastic surgery can do

Sarah's big nose was now small and neat
Huge-breasted Laura could now see her feet
Curvaceous Sue who once chuckled with glee
Now was stick-thin and frowned constantly

Old personalities still floundered through
Multicoloured hair and facelifts new
There were only a few originals like me
Who'd had no money so had to let things be

Torrid affairs were discussed with flair
Needless to say I was the quietest there
Next they talked about holidays, houses and men
They heard little from me again

I'll give the next reunion a miss for sure
Another non-participating role I'll not endure
Even if my life becomes filled with glamour
Reunion nerves would make me stammer.

Joyce Atkinson

HIGH FUNCTION

When I was a lad I climbed Scafell
Helvellyn and Skiddaw as well
I wore big boots and a large rucksack
As I clambered over Saddleback

An excursion over Maiden Moor
Was far more than I bargained for
'Cause I was taken short alas
And the only toilet tissue was some long, damp grass

On Maiden Moor I made such a pile
The aroma could be smelt on top of High Stile
But the wind and rain came to my aid
And the terrible stench began to fade

From Dale Head High Spy and High Seat
No evidence was spotted of my feat
So I strode off to Watendlath
Stripped off my smelly raiment and jumped in the bath

So fellsmen all whoever you may be
A call of nature can be tragedy
Take heed of my warning when you're out for a walk
And get yourself a nice tight-fitting cork

Or trap your shirt between your legs
To curtail all those wayward dregs
For diarrhoea can give you hell
When you hike across Great Gable or the top of Bowfell.

Terence Leslie

The Avocado

Today I received an avocado
it was in one of those offers - you see
but not the one that says
buy one get one free

I turned to an assistant, who was standing nearby
'What can I do with an avocado?' I said with a sigh
'You see I've just acquired one free.'
I got a blank expression and the words, 'That's news to me.'

I looked at the avocado in my shopping basket small
asked another assistant
who said they were not adventurous at all

Now I've never had an avocado
I like my fruit plain
bananas, apples, peaches
I look on others with disdain

I like strawberries, raspberries, cherries galore
then I had a thought, when I get my avocado home
I'll ask my neighbour next door

At home I asked my neighbour
what could I do with my avocado so
she stared and shrugged her shoulders and pronounced, 'I dunno'

So my avocado sits in the fruit bowl - wow
with a small sticky notelet attached
saying, 'What can I do with an avocado,
will someone tell me now?'

Katherine Parker

OH! INNOCENCE

'Dad, can I have an increase in my weekly pocket cash?
I want to move into the shed and live with Molly Nash.'
'I think you're rather young for that you are both not even nine,
there are still many years to go - then sign the dotted line.'

'If my allowance is increased to twelve pounds every year -
plus Molly's five pounds fifty we'll just manage - with no beer.'
'What if a little one should come along, you two will then be three.'
'We've thought of that as well, Dad - so far we've been *luck-ee*.'

Jim Pritchard

A Light Shower

Richard Jones in a hotel one day
Had a shower that stuck down half way,
So he just washed his feet
And the rest he left neat . . .
And then wondered why friends moved away!

Margaret Carter

JOHNNY BULL

Johnny Bull sits next to me at school,
he sniffs and snorts like Chief Sitting Bull.
Soap and water he's never seen and the
mess in his ears is a sight, believe me.

His nose is constantly running
and never a tissue does he use,
he just sniffs it all back up,
swallows hard, then starts again.

I don't know what he eats for breakfast,
it can't be at all very healthy,
the smell that emits from his
mouth and his bum, only proves to me
that it's lethal.

PE I must dread the most,
for then he takes off his shoes.
The stench from his socks
is a hell of a shock,
and makes me feel quite dizzy.

Now I'm quite looking forward to swimming,
Johnny Bull, I'm sure is not,
for he hates the sight of water,
at least he'll get a wash.

Jane Margaret Isaac

ELDERBERRY WINE

I paid a visit to dear Old Aunt
She lived near the village green
Knocking on the door, she called
'Come in and sample my elderberry wine.'
Tipple after tipple and going quite dizzy
I thought I had better go home,
Mounting my cycle and riding criss-cross all over the lane,
Mother wasn't pleased and said, 'Where have you been?'
'I've been to Old Aunt's on Springfield Green.'
'I will have words with her, leading a young girl astray.'
I have never touched elderberry wine since that day.

Olive M Poole

JENNY HEN

Jenny Hen was quite a bird
On Farmer Andrew's farm.
Fried or boiled or scrambled,
Her eggs were in demand.
Until one day she laid one
With a shell too hard to break.
No hammer, file or chisel
Could win. Was it a fake?
A scientist decided
To analyse the shell,
And found that it was solid,
Could Jenny then be well?
They found that she had swallowed
A marble in her food
And was relieved by passing
It in this manner, who'd
Have guessed she never choked?
It seemed that marble grew so big
She laid it with relief and heard
A loud grunt from Tim Pig,
'That landed on my trotter!
It really is no joke,
Your eggs go well with bacon
When you lay them with a yoke.'

Marion Skelton

Yorkshire Pudding

Riding down to Hornsea,
A signpost we espied,
It bore a funny legend
That sent us goggle-eyed!

'This way to Sigglethorne.'
Oh! What thoughts went swirling round,
Laughs and giggles were airborne,
Then suddenly, no sound!

Should siggle be squiggle?
And do siggles have thorns?
Can a siggle then wriggle
When thorns its tail adorns?

Living with that place name,
I'd get out of the groove.
Silly Sigglethorne, goodbye!
To Wetwang I would move.

Evelyn Balmain

ANCHOR BOOKS SUBMISSIONS INVITED
SOMETHING FOR EVERYONE

ANCHOR BOOKS GEN - Any subject, light-hearted clean fun, nothing unprintable please.

THE OPPOSITE SEX - Have your say on the opposite gender. Do they drive you mad or can we co-exist in harmony?

THE NATURAL WORLD - Are we destroying the world around us? What should we do to preserve the beauty and the future of our planet - you decide!

All poems no longer than 30 lines.
Always welcome! No fee!
Plus cash prizes to be won!

Mark your envelope (eg *The Natural World*)
And send to:
Anchor Books
Remus House, Coltsfoot Drive
Peterborough, PE2 9JX

OVER £10,000 IN POETRY PRIZES TO BE WON!

Send an SAE for details on our New Year 2003 competition!